## Turbulent Planet

# Wild Water

## Floods

Tony Allan

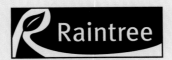

**www.raintreepublishers.co.uk**
Visit our website to find out more information about **Raintree** books.

To order:
☎ Phone 44 (0) 1865 888113
▤ Send a fax to 44 (0) 1865 314091
▢ Visit the Raintree Bookshop at **www.raintreepublishers.co.uk** to browse our catalogue and order online.

First published in Great Britain by Raintree, Halley Court, Jordan Hill, Oxford OX2 8EJ, part of Harcourt Education. Raintree is a registered trademark of Harcourt Education Ltd.

Produced for Raintree by Discovery Books Ltd

Editorial: Saskia Besier, Melanie Copland and Carol Usher
Design: Michelle Lisseter and Rob Norridge
Illustrations: Peter Bull and Stefan Chabluk
Picture Research: Rachel Tisdale
Consultant: Keith Lye
Production: Duncan Gilbert
Printed and bound in China and Hong Kong by South China Printing Company
Originated by Repro Multi Warna

ISBN 1 844 43624 1
08 07 06 05 04
10 9 8 7 6 5 4 3 2 1

**British Library Cataloguing in Publication Data**
Allan, Tony
Wild water : floods – (Turbulent planet)
1. Floods – Juvenile literature 2. Natural disasters – Juvenile literature
551.4'89

A full catalogue record for this book is available from the British Library.

**Photo acknowledgements**
p.4/5, Corbis/Philip Wallick; p.5 top, Science Photo Library/ Dr Morley Read; p.5 middle, Corbis/Ecoscene/Sally A Morgan; p.5 bottom, Corbis/Micheal Nicholson; p.6/7, Science Photo Library/Simon Fraser; p.7, Corbis/Patrick Ward; p.8, Corbis/Yann Arthus-Bertrand; p.9, Corbis/ Reuters; p.10, Science Photo Library/Alan Sirulnikoff; p.11, Corbis/Carl & Ann Purcell; p.12/13, Corbis/Caroline Penn; p.12, Corbis Sygma/Bonifacio; p.13, Science Photo Library/ Dr Morley Read ; p.14, Corbis/Charlie Munsey; p.14/15, Corbis/Bettmann; p.15, Science Photo Library/Dr Morley Read; p.16, Science Photo Library/John Mead; p.17, Corbis/Bettmann; p.18/19, Corbis/Ecoscene/Sally A Morgan; p.18, Corbis/Cordaiy Photo Library/Chris North; p.19, Corbis/Lloyd Cluff p.20/21, Corbis/Eye Ubiquitous/Julia Waterlow; p.20, NHPA/Daniel Heuclin; p.21, Corbis/ Wolfgang Kaehler; p.22/23, Corbis/Micheal Nicholson; p.23, Science Photo Library/Douglas Faulkner; p.24, Corbis; p.24 left, Corbis/Connie Ricca; p.25, Corbis; p.26/27, Corbis/Australia/News Ltd; p.26, Reuters; p.27, Corbis/ Wolfgang Kaehler; p.28, Corbis/Stocktrek; p.28 left, Corbis Sygma/Bill Alkofer; p.29, Corbis/Jacques Torregano; p.30/31, Corbis/Patrick Robert; p.30, Corbis Sygma/Silva Joao; p.31, Corbis Sygma/Las Vegas Sun/Sam Morris; p.32, Corbis/Reuters/Edy Regar; p.33, Corbis/Bisson Bernard; p.33 right, Corbis/Icone Films/Gilles Fonlupt; p.34, Science Photo Library/Andy Harmer; p.34 left, Corbis/Kent News & Picture; p.35, Corbis/Eye Ubiquitous/Jex David Cole; p.36/37, Corbis/Charles E. Rotkin; p.37, Corbis; p.38/39, Philip Gould; p.39 top, Science Photo Library/NASA/ Goddard Flight Center; p.39 bottom, Corbis/FK Photo; p.40/41, Corbis/George H H Huey; p.40, Science Photo Library/NASA/R B Husar; p.41, Corbis Sygma/Telegram Tribune/Jason Mellom; p.42/43, Chromosohm/Joseph Sohm; p.42, Corbis Sygma/Kent News & Picture; p.43, Corbis/Robert Essel NYC; p.44, Corbis/Micheal Nicholson; p.45, Corbis/Reuters/Edy Regar.

Cover photograph reproduced with permission of Topham/Picture Point

# Contents

Any words appearing in the text in bold, **like this**, are explained in the Glossary. You can also look out for them in the Wet words box at the bottom of each page.

# Rising waters

> **Water** is coming down the back garden! The wall is **breaking!**

The last words spoken by Fred Floyd. He was killed in a flood in Lynmouth, UK, in August 1952.

It has been raining for days. The river is higher than anyone can remember. The local radio station is **broadcasting** warnings: 'Heavy rains will continue into the night. There will be flooding in some areas.'

Darkness falls. The only sound is the splashing of raindrops on the roof and windows. Suddenly the lights go out throughout the house. The street lamps outside are dark, the electricity must be cut off. In the gloom, all you can see is the rising water. There is just enough time to get upstairs. You must hurry to keep above the rising **torrent**.

A river floods across a road in California, USA, after a storm in January 1999. ▷

broadcast  give out information on the radio, television or the Internet

## Find out later...

**What causes floods?**

**Can floods sometimes be helpful?**

**What can people do to stop floods?**

## Flood fears

Every year, floods affect hundreds of thousands of people around the world. They can strike almost anywhere. Often there is very little warning and they can be deadly. The International Red Cross reports that floods killed 318,000 people between 1991 and 1995. These floods drove more than 1.5 billion people from their homes.

During a flood the water and mud gets into everything. It costs billions of dollars to repair the damage caused by floods.

torrent   powerful flow of water

# Wild waters

### In the flood zone

Floods can happen anywhere if more than the usual amount of rain falls. But some parts of the world are more likely to flood than other areas. Regions that often flood and places mentioned in this book are marked on this map.

## Water out of control

Floods occur when water spreads out over dry land. The most common cause of flooding is when rivers burst their banks. This happens because heavy rain fills rivers and they overflow.

There are other reasons too. **Dams** hold back water in **reservoirs**. If dams give way, a wall of water crashes down on to the valleys below. **Landslides** can block the course of streams, forcing the water out of its usual path. In some countries, ice and snow high up in the mountains melt in the summer. This **meltwater** raises the water level in rivers, just like too much rain does.

Alaska

Canada

Netherlands

France

USA

Italy

Huang He River

Mount Shasta

Pennsylvania

Mississippi River

Tigris River

Brahmaputra River

Japan

California

Grand Canyon

Colorado

Galveston

Gulf of Mexico

Euphrate River

Indus

Ganges

Yang tze River

Kansas

Mexico

Egypt

Bangladesh

Red River

Vietnam

PACIFIC OCEAN

Hawaiian Islands

Honduras

Caribbean Sea

Nile River

Chao Phraya River

Mekong River

PACIFIC OCEAN

Ecuador

Somalia

Kenya

Papua New Guinea

Peru

Amazon River

Indonesia

Java

South Africa

Australia

**Wet words**    hurricane   huge swirling storm with winds of more than 118 kilometres (73 miles) per hour

## Invaded by the sea

The sea can easily sweep over **low-lying**, coastal plains. Whipped by **hurricane**-force winds, it can **surge** over the coastline. Some of the world's coasts are often hit by big storms. One stretch of the Atlantic coast is known as 'Hurricane Alley' because it sees so many hurricanes. This area includes the Caribbean Sea and the east coast of the USA. Hurricane-related floods in the USA caused almost US $8 billion of damage in the 1990s.

Some of the very worst sea floods have nothing to do with winds. **Tsunamis** cause them. These are giant waves caused by **earthquakes** and volcanic eruptions on the seabed. They can drown whole towns and villages.

This flood barrier protects low coastal lands in the Netherlands. ▽

### Ice jams

Ice jams can cause floods when frozen rivers start to melt. Chunks of floating ice pile up at bridges and in narrow stretches. These block the river's flow and cause it to overflow its banks.

### Land from the sea

Almost one fifth of the Netherlands was once under water. It still would be if people had not built high walls, called **dykes**. These keep the sea out. The people use this land for farming, industry and housing.

reservoir   artificial or natural lake that stores water for people to use
tsunami   giant wave set off by an undersea earthquake or volcanic eruption

7

## River action

A river starts as a small stream high above sea level. Its starting point is called its **source**. When rain falls, some of the rainwater seeps into the ground and some flows over the surface. The water collects into small streams, which come together to form a river. Near the start of a river, the slopes are steep and so the water has a lot of energy. The running water washes away rocks, soil and plants from the river's bed and banks. This is called **erosion**. The river can carry a lot of material because it is fast flowing.

River water spills out over a flood plain after heavy rain in the Kakadu National Park, north Australia. ▽

### Where has all the water come from?

When there are heavy rains, the rivers collect the extra water. The water level gradually rises. Floods happen when the water level is higher than the riverbank. This often happens a long way from the river's source, in the flat lands near its mouth.

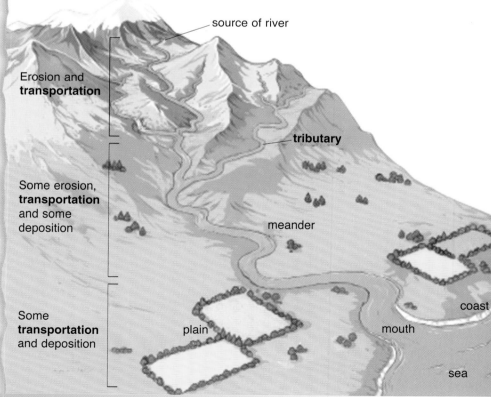

source of river

Erosion and **transportation**

**tributary**

Some erosion, **transportation** and some deposition

meander

Some **transportation** and deposition

plain

mouth

coast

sea

cyclone   name given to a hurricane in the southern hemisphere
meander   bend in the course of a river

## Lower down the river

As the river flows downstream, the ground begins to flatten out. The river flows more slowly and has less energy. The water cannot transport large **particles**, but the river still holds many smaller particles such as **silt** and clay. Here the path of the river goes from side to side. Over many years, the **meanders** wear away the valley sides, making the bottom flat. If the river floods, this flat area of land will be covered with water. It is called a flood **plain**.

## Near the sea

As the river moves to the sea it flows slowly and does not have much energy. It may drop even the smallest particles. This is called **deposition**. Close to its **mouth** the river may have extremely gentle valley sides, big meanders and a wide flood plain. When the river floods the water covers a huge area.

### At risk from rivers and sea

Bangladesh in southern Asia is especially threatened by flooding. Most of the country is on a low-lying plain. Two of the world's great rivers, the Ganges and the Brahmaputra, meet here. The coast is often hit by **cyclones** too.

A family in Bangladesh seeks safety on a raft during floods in 2000. ▽

**mouth**   where a river flows into the sea
**transportation**   when material is carried by water or wind

## Water under the ground

When rain falls on land, some of it sinks down through the soil into the rocks below. It seeps through tiny holes or cracks in the rock. When it reaches a solid, compact rock, it can go no farther, so it often bubbles to the surface as a spring, the **source** of a river.

## Water on the move

Water is always on the move. Since the Earth began, billions of years ago, water has moved from the sea to the land and back again. This is a non-stop process known as the **water cycle**.

## Water to clouds

The sun heats up the air and the surface water in oceans, rivers and lakes. Some water **evaporates**, turning into **water vapour**, which behaves like a gas. Warm air rises because it is light. As it rises, the air cools. Soon, the invisible water vapour in the air **condenses** to form visible water droplets or ice **crystals**. Huge amounts of water droplets and ice crystals form clouds in the sky. The droplets and ice crystals grow in size as they merge together. They eventually fall back as rain, snow or hail. This is called **precipitation**.

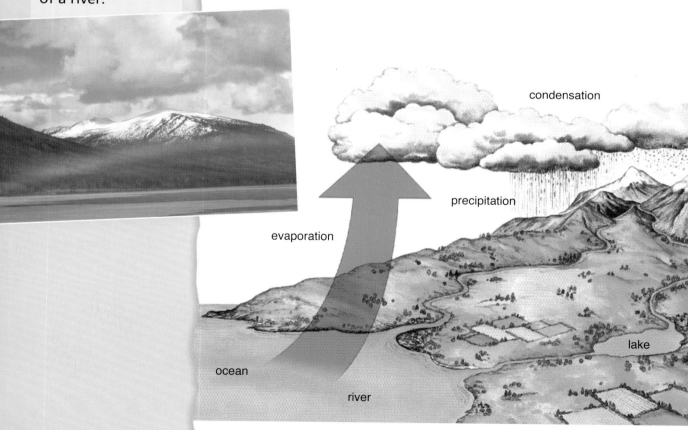

condensation

precipitation

evaporation

ocean

river

lake

condense   when a gas turns into a liquid
evaporate   when a liquid turns into a gas

## Down to earth

Some rain falls straight back into the seas and oceans. The rest falls on land, where it soaks into the soil and underlying rocks. This is called **groundwater**. Plants take up some of this water through their roots. Water evaporates from the leaves of plants into the air too. This is called **transpiration**.

High up near its source China's mighty Huang He (Yellow River) is still quite a small stream. It breaks up into several channels to pass through a mountain valley. ▽

## The water table

When water soaks into the ground it is called groundwater. This water fills spaces in the rock or soil above the **bedrock**. The water table is the top level of the groundwater. After heavy rain the water table rises. If it rises above the surface of the ground it becomes a flood.

transpiration  when plants give off water vapour through their leaves
water vapour   water in the form of a gas

# When rivers burst their banks

Heavy rainfall is the most common cause of river floods. Rainwater soaks into the ground. Some water is held in the soil, but the rest flows into **tributaries**. The **volume** of water in the river increases as the tributaries join the main river. Finally the water level rises too high and the river bursts its banks. This may be hundreds of kilometres farther downstream.

The Mekong Delta region of Vietnam, South-east Asia, often floods. ▽

## Water in the cities

Today much of the ground is covered with concrete and tarmac. When rain falls on these areas it cannot go into the ground. The water flows straight into rivers and risk of flooding is much greater.

catchment area   area of land drained by a river
monsoon   rainy season in some tropical countries

When ice and snow melts in hilly areas, the water level of rivers rises. In the northern states of the USA in 1996 and 1997, mild air caused the snow and ice in the mountains to melt. There was severe flooding. Over 50 people died and the damage cost more than US $5 billion.

Rivers flood all around the world, but some of the worst flooding happens in southern Asia. Winds called **monsoons** bring heavy rains in summer and autumn. The rains swell great rivers like the Ganges, the Brahmaputra and the Mekong. In 2000, monsoon rains in the Mekong valley caused terrible floods. Four and a half million people had to leave their homes.

## Cutting down forests

Trees and plants take up water from the ground. When they are chopped down the water runs into rivers instead. This increases the amount of water in rivers. They are more likely to flood.

## Catchment areas

All the water that drains into a river is collected in a river's **catchment area**. Catchment areas can be huge. The Amazon River in South America drains an area of land over 7 million square kilometres. This area is nearly 30 times the size of Britain.

---

**tributary**  small river flowing into a larger one
**volume**  amount of space taken up by a solid, liquid or gas

## Flash flood

Sometimes rivers flood after weeks of steady rain. At other times **cloudbursts** can make them run over their banks in hours. If a river floods six hours or less after rain starts to fall, it is called a **flash flood**. These floods are often the most dangerous, because people cannot get out of the danger area in time.

## Fast and furious

Sometimes victims are caught by surprise. In August 1999, a group of 44 people were **canyoning** down a river in Switzerland. Twenty-one of them were killed by an unexpected raging **torrent**. Two years earlier, 11 hikers drowned when a 3 metre wall of water swept them away. They had been walking through Antelope Canyon in the Grand Canyon National Park, USA.

◁ Antelope Canyon in Grand Canyon National Park, USA, is normally very dry.

canyoning   sport of climbing and swimming up or down gorges
cloudburst   sudden heavy rainstorm

## Wall of water

One of the USA's worst flash floods happened in Colorado, in 1976. The state was enjoying a long holiday weekend. Holidaymakers flocked to the Big Thompson Canyon. This is a steep-sided **gorge** 40 kilometres long. On 31 July a terrible storm struck the region. After four hours of torrential rain, a wall of water **surged** down the canyon. It travelled faster than people could run. The **death toll** was 139 people.

Floodwater rushes down the Mazan Valley, high in the Andes Mountains of Ecuador. In normal times this stream is only 2 metres wide.
▽

## Flood fact

Driving away from a flood can be a dangerous thing to do. In the USA, half of the people killed by recent flash floods were swept away in their cars.

**True or false?**

Flash floods only happen in the countryside.

Answer: False.

Built-up areas are especially at risk. Water flows through city streets and over parking lots. A flash flood killed 25 people in Kansas City, USA, in 1977.

A rescue worker looks at the damage done by the Big Thompson River flash
◁ flood in Colorado, USA, in 1976.

**death toll** number of people who died
**flash flood** quickly developing flood

## Broken dams

A **dam** will be strong enough to hold back the water behind it, if it is well designed. But tragic accidents still occur. When dams burst they release great walls of water. These wipe out everything in their path. Often they happen because of **flaws** in the dam. The **foundations** may give way. Water may get into tiny cracks in the dam and weaken it. The dam might not be able to hold back the force of water after heavy rains. Fortunately this happens rarely. Nowadays there are strict government rules about dams in most countries. These make sure dams are safe.

Embankment dam

Gravity dam

Arch dam

Buttress dam

Mount Shasta Dam in California, USA. Dams are important for controlling floods and providing a reliable source of water.

### Types of dam

There are four main types of dam. Most dams are embankment dams. They are used in rivers that have broad valleys. Gravity, arch and buttress dams are found in narrow valleys. Arch dams are cheaper than gravity dams. Buttress dams are better in areas where earthquakes are likely.

dam    barrier built to hold back water
flaw    fault or weakness

## Too much rain

At 3:10 pm on 31 May 1889, in the US state of Pennsylvania, the South Fork Dam collapsed after heavy rains. Behind it lay a huge **reservoir**. The **torrent** poured on to the mining town of Johnstown. The town was demolished. A total of 2209 people died in the Johnstown flood.

## Landslide

Natural events such as **landslides** and **earthquakes** can cause dam disasters. In 1963, the side of a mountain slid into the reservoir behind Italy's Vaiont Dam. This made a wave of water 100 metres high. The giant wave swept over the top of the dam and into the valley below. It killed 2600 people.

> " The dam is breaking! Run for your lives! "
>
> Engineer John G. Parke, 1889. He rode on horseback to warn people when the South Fork Dam was about to break.

Shattered houses hit by the floodwater in the Vaiont Dam disaster in Italy in 1963.

foundations   heavy base that a building stands on
landslide   rocks and earth sliding down a hillside

# Helpful floods

Most people think of floods as bad, yet sometimes they can have good effects. For many centuries, Egypt's River Nile regularly burst its banks in late summer. It flooded the land on either side of the river and **deposited silt** on the land. The Nile had carried this from the hills near its **source**. The silt contains **mineral nutrients**. These are important for plants to grow well. The land on either side of the Nile became **fertile**, producing bumper harvests of crops. People called the Nile Valley the Black Land, from the colour of its rich soil. The land beyond the flood zone, known as the Red Land, remained desert.

### Ancient civilizations

Many **civilizations** developed near great rivers. This is because the land on either side was fertile and it was easy to produce food. This was the case in the Indus Valley, now called Pakistan.

A canal brings water from the River Nile to ▽ fields in Egypt.

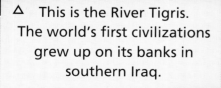

△ This is the River Tigris. The world's first civilizations grew up on its banks in southern Iraq.

civilization   well-developed social system
fertilizer   chemical that gives plants substances necessary for growth

## Floods and food

Today too, millions of farmers depend on regular floods. They control the floods to help them earn a living. Rice growers in southern Asia use flooded fields called **paddies** to grow their crops. This is because rice seedlings grow best when covered with water. The best land for rice paddies is in the flood **plains** of great rivers, like the Red River in Vietnam and the Chao Phraya in Thailand. These rivers often overflow their banks and flood the fields.

### No floods, no nutrients

Farmers in the Nile Valley now have to use artificial **fertilizer** to provide plants with nutrients and minerals. But the plants do not use all of the fertilizer and some is washed into the rivers. This has **polluted** the Nile's waters.

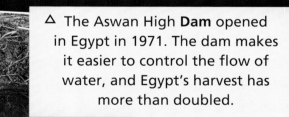

△ The Aswan High **Dam** opened in Egypt in 1971. The dam makes it easier to control the flow of water, and Egypt's harvest has more than doubled.

**mineral**   natural, solid substance that does not come from an animal or plant
**polluted**   dirty, containing harmful substances

## The Yellow River

More people live near the banks of the Huang He (Yellow River) in China than any other river. The land is very **fertile** because of the rich yellow **silt**. This gave the river its name. The yellow silt comes from a special kind of soil, called loess. Near its **source**, the river **erodes** the river's bed and banks. It transports the yellow silt far downstream.

## Mud and floods

The Huang He (Yellow River) is special for another reason. It floods more than any other river on Earth. This is due to its very muddy water. Some of the silt sinks to the bottom. This raises the level of the riverbed and the water level gets close to the top of the riverbank.

For many centuries, people have tried to hold the river by building **dykes**. They have had to rebuild the dykes many times, each time building them higher. The riverbed is now 4.5 metres above the surrounding **plain** in some places. When a dyke gives way, a huge **volume** of water spills on to the land. The resulting floods are terrible.

## Sorghum

The Chinese have used a plant called sorghum to help control floods for a very long time. Tied in bundles, its tightly bunched roots trap the silt. Millions of bundles are built into the sides of the dykes. They stop erosion of the riverbank by the river.

dyke   long wall of earth built to keep water out
fertile   soil that can grow good crops

## China's sorrow

When the river floods the water spreads out for hundreds of miles. The floodwaters **deposit** silt over the surrounding farmland and make it fertile. However these floods can also kill thousands of people. Almost a million people died when the Yellow River flooded in 1887. Although this river makes China rich, it is known as 'China's sorrow'.

△ The rice fields on the banks of China's Yangtze River are built up as terraces. They stop water draining away after floods.

**silt** soil particles carried in a river
**stranded** stuck, or washed aground

# When the sea floods the land

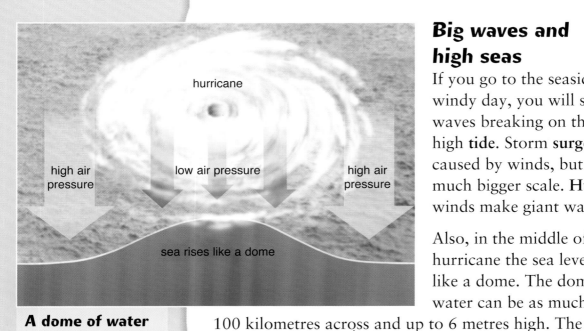

hurricane

high air pressure

low air pressure

high air pressure

sea rises like a dome

## Big waves and high seas

If you go to the seaside on a windy day, you will see big waves breaking on the shore at high **tide**. Storm **surges** are also caused by winds, but on a much bigger scale. **Hurricane** winds make giant waves.

Also, in the middle of a hurricane the sea level rises like a dome. The dome of water can be as much as 100 kilometres across and up to 6 metres high. The combination of high tides, big waves and raised sea level can be enough to sweep over the best **coastal defences**.

## A dome of water

The **air pressure** is less in the centre of a hurricane than the air pressure farther out. This means air presses less heavily on that area of water – and the water rises. This raised sea level contributes to a terrifying storm surge.

The Thames Barrier on ▷ the River Thames in London.

coastal defence   system to protect the coast from the sea
low-lying   land that is very close to or below the level of the sea

# Be prepared!

Sea floods are most common along tropical shores because they are often hit by hurricanes. But any **low-lying coastal** region can be at risk. One of the worst storm surges of recent times was in the North Sea in January 1953. It raised the sea level by 2.3 metres. In eastern England, 307 people died and 22,000 were made homeless as the sea swept over the land. In the Netherlands, 1800 people drowned.

After that disaster the Dutch launched the Delta Project. This involved building **dams** and **dykes**. The Delta Project took almost 50 years to complete. The English built the world's largest movable flood barrier on the River Thames. This was to protect the capital city of London.

## U.S. disaster

A hurricane caused a storm surge in September 1900. This hit Galveston, Texas, and killed over 6,000 people, making it the worst disaster in the history of the USA.

**surge**   sudden rush of water
**tide**   regular rising and falling of the sea. This happens twice a day.

23

## Tsunamis

**Tsunami** means 'harbour waves' in Japanese. They are also known as 'tidal waves'. In fact they have nothing to do with **tides**. Undersea **earthquakes, landslides** or volcanic eruptions on the ocean floor cause the huge waves. They travel for hundreds of kilometres through the ocean as small waves less than a metre high. But they build up in size as they get near land. By the time they reach the shore, they tower over the seafront.

## Killer waves

The power of tsunamis can be terrible. They can crush houses and throw ships hundreds of metres inland. In 1896, a tsunami struck Japan and killed about 27,000 people. When the Krakatoa volcano erupted in 1883, it caused a tidal wave. This hit the Pacific islands of Java and Sumatra. Its waves reached 35 metres high and swept away at least 36,000 people. This tsunami killed more people and caused more damage than any other we know about.

**Flood fact: stay off the beach**

Never go to a beach to watch a tsunami arrive. By the time you see the wave, it will be too late to escape.

Flooding caused by a tsunami in 1957 sweeps over coastal land on Oahu, one of the Hawaiian islands. ▽

TSUNAMI HAZARD ZONE

IN CASE OF EARTHQUAKE, GO TO HIGH GROUND OR INLAND

fault line   crack in the Earth's crust
satellite   object that moves around the Earth in space

## Tsunami warning

In the past tsunamis struck unexpectedly. Now there are specially built centres that watch out for signs a tsunami might happen. The centres are near the Pacific Ocean, where earthquakes are common under the sea. The Pacific Tsunami Warning System has headquarters in Hawaii and Alaska. Scientists study the information from computers and **satellites** around the clock. At the first sign of undersea shock waves, warnings are given to the threatened areas. This way the killer waves do not take people by surprise.

## The monster of Lituya Bay

The Tlingit people used to hunt in Lituya Bay, Alaska. They had a story about a fearful monster. This lived in an underwater cavern, near the bay's mouth. When angry, it would thrash around in fury. Terrible storms sometimes swept the usually peaceful inlet and this story explained them.

### The mystery solved

Scientists found a **fault line** in the seabed, across the entrance of Lituya Bay. This causes earthquakes. Earthquakes can send tsunamis crashing towards the shore.

The tsunami that struck Seward, Alaska, in 1964 wrecked this oil tanker and fishing boat. ▷

tide   regular rising and falling of the sea. This happens twice a day.
tsunami   giant wave set off by an undersea earthquake or volcanic eruption

## Papua New Guinea, 1998

Warning systems help to reduce the threat from **tsunamis** but they have not removed it. Sometimes the killer waves build up too fast to give any warnings. Then the effects are terrible.

On 17 July 1998, people living in Papua New Guinea felt the shock of a strong **earthquake**. Just 15 minutes later, three huge waves struck the **coast**. The biggest of them was 15 metres high. The villages of Arop and Warupu suffered the most. All the buildings were destroyed and two out of every three people died. In total, the tsunami killed 2600 people. Out of all the tsunamis in recent years, this killed the most people.

**Flood fact: gas powered?**

Survivors of the Papua New Guinea tsunami descibed the wave as hot and smelly. Scientists think that undersea gas may have escaped into the water from the earthquake.

Survivors check the damage done by the tsunami that struck Papua New Guinea in July 1998.  ▽

On the anniversary of  △ the Papua New Guinea 1998 tsunami, people remember their friends and family who died.

eyewitness   person who can tell about an event from personal experience
lagoon   lake connected to the sea

## How it was

Before the tsunami struck, **eyewitnesses** heard a loud booming noise. Then there was a roaring sound, like a low-flying aeroplane. The sea went back about 50 metres from the shore. The undersea earthquake was sucking water down before pushing it back out. Fish and crabs were left **stranded**. The water grew hot and seemed to bubble.

Then the first wave came. There was almost no time to escape. A few people scrambled up trees. The wave flung lucky **survivors** on to soft ground or into a nearby **lagoon**. The unlucky ones drowned or were battered against rocks or trees. One baby had a very lucky escape. When the giant waves finally rolled back, the baby was found floating on the torn-off roof of a house.

First I saw the sea on the horizon rise and explode, sending spray high in the air. Then there was a sound like distant thunder.

John Sanawe, who lived through the disaster, describing the first signs of the tsunami.

A lagoon in Papua △ New Guinea in calm weather.

survivor   person who escapes death

# How to survive a flood

> I am lucky it's not worse. This is a small problem compared with what others in this town are facing.
>
> George Cariveau,
> 24 April, 1997,
> North Dakota,
> USA.

## Flood alert

Floods are as dangerous as ever. But today people are better at **forecasting** them. Weather forecasters receive reports from **weather stations** on the ground. They also use **satellites** and specially equipped aeroplanes. These track storms that might cause flooding. When a flood looks likely, radio and television stations give out flood alerts. These warn people in the area about the danger.

A satellite photo tracks the position of a **hurricane** in the Gulf of Mexico, east of Florida, in 1996. ▽

△ George Cariveau looks down at about half a metre of water. This is in his son's basement bedroom at his home in Grand Forks.

forecast   give information about something that might happen
monitor   check something regularly

# Measuring flood risk

There are other ways to check the risk of flooding. Special instruments **monitor** the state of rivers. They are automatic and are on 24 hours a day. Water-depth instruments measure how high the water is. They are usually set up on the riverbank and connected to the river by a pipe. If they were put in midstream they might get swept away. Other instruments check how fast the river is flowing. The machines send the information to computers. Then experts study the findings. There are over 7,000 monitors in the USA alone. They are run by the United States Geological Survey.

Some laboratories have special equipment for studying floodwater. These work out how much rain will cause flooding in different places.

## Underground is underwater

In towns there is a risk of flooding. Keep out of basements, underpasses or storm drains, they are are the most dangerous places to be. This is because they fill up with water first and it is difficult to escape from them.

Research workers check the flow of the River Seine in Paris. They are looking out for rising water levels. ▽

weather station    base for recording the weather

## Survival tips

If you know a flood is coming, get away from the danger zone fast. If you get trapped, taking these steps might keep you safe:

- Inside your home, prepare a **survival** kit
- Warn everyone in the house about the danger
- Do your best to warn neighbours
- An adult needs to turn off the gas, electricity and water supplies
- Move your valuables to an upper storey of the house
- When the waters enter the house, keep moving upwards.

### Survival kit

If you know a flood might be coming, store these vital supplies somewhere safe and dry.

Things to take:
- ✓ Torch, plus batteries
- ✓ Battery-operated radio
- ✓ First-aid kit
- ✓ Food
- ✓ Drinking water
- ✓ Tin opener
- ✓ Medicines
- ✓ Warm, dry clothes

Rescue workers in Mozambique help a 73-year-old man to safety in March 2000. He had climbed a tree to escape flood waters. ▽

After storms in the south of France in 1999, a man waits for rescue on the roof of his flooded home. ▷

electrocute   pass electricity through the body

## If you are outside

Never stay in a car or allow someone to drive through floods. Just 30 centimetres of water can sweep small cars away. Do not try to walk through a flood. Fast flowing water only 15 centimetres deep can carry you off. Watch out for fallen power lines as they might still be live. Electricity passes easily through water and you could be **electrocuted**.

The most important thing to remember is to try to get as high up as you can. This could be on a hillside, up a building or a tree. Do not try to swim to safety unless you have to. Instead wait to be rescued.

**True or false?**

A car is a safe place to sit out a flood.

Answer: False.

Out of 364 people killed by floods in the USA between 1998 and 2002, 206 were in cars, trucks or other vehicles.

△ Flood waters carry off a car in Las Vegas, USA, in July 1999.

## Keeping alive

Often more people die after the floods go down than in the flood itself. Thousands of people may be left homeless and without shelter. Getting help can be difficult. This is because the floodwater may have destroyed roads and bridges. It could have brought down telephone and power lines.

## No food or water

The floods might have destroyed crops and drowned farm animals. People could starve. In **developing countries**, **famine** often follows a flood. Water is often too dirty to drink because drains and **sewers** can overflow into drinking water supplies. Sewage or chemicals from farms or factories often **pollute** the floodwater itself. Floodwater can also spread diseases.

△ People left homeless after a flood swept through their village in Sumatra in 2003. At least 150 people were killed.

emergency services   police, fire and ambulance services
famine   long-term shortage of food

## No heat or light

Even in wealthy **developed countries**, flooding leaves a huge job for the **emergency services**. Homeless people need shelter and food. Damaged gas pipes and electricity cables can cause fires. Engineers have to repair power lines before homes can have their light and heating restored.

## Operation clean up

Cleaning up after the floods go down is a long and messy job. Streets are often covered in deep mud and need washing down. Rooms of flooded houses are ruined and people have to replace items damaged by the water.

### When the waters go down

- Only return home when it is safe.

- Throw out all food and medicines, if they have been in contact with floodwater.

- Do not drink tap water until you are told it is safe to do so.

- Check for gas leaks from broken pipes.

- Be careful of electrical wires and fittings. They could be live.

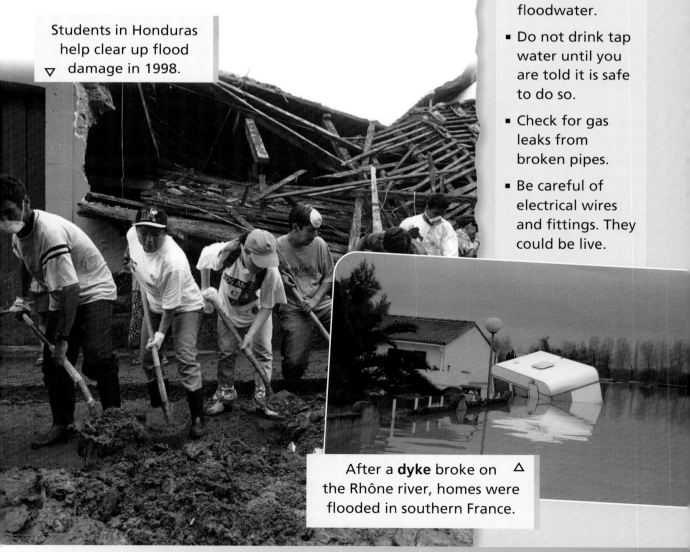

Students in Honduras help clear up flood damage in 1998. ▽

After a **dyke** broke on △ the Rhône river, homes were flooded in southern France.

**sewer**  large undergound pipe for carrying away waste water

# Coping with floods

## Preventing floods

People have always tried to protect themselves from floods. This usually means raising the height of the riverbanks to hold back rising water. They often use mounds of earth or stone to do this. Theses are called **embankments** or **levees**.

People build **dams** to control the flow of rivers. Dams can also help steer the river away from towns and villages. Sometimes they dig **diversion channels** to carry off part of the stream. Rivers can be widened in places. Then they can carry more water.

## Looking after the land

Good farming methods can help stop flooding. Farmers can dig ditches and keep them clear. Ditches drain unwanted water from fields. They can plant trees and bushes on hillsides. The trees help slow down the flow of rainwater and they also take some of it up with their roots.

### Be prepared

Take out **insurance** to cover damage to your house and contents. Use sandbags to block up doors and windows. Sand soaks up water and helps to floodproof the home.

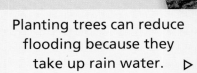

Planting trees can reduce flooding because they take up rain water.  ▷

diversion channel   channel dug alongside a river to drain floodwater
insurance   agreement to provide money in case of a disaster

## Getting away

People do their best to escape floods, if they cannot stop them. In southern Africa, when cattle herders know the Zambezi River is about to flood, they move their cattle to high ground. In the lowlands of southern Asia many houses are built on **stilts**. These raise them above the floods. When the Ganges and Brahmaputra rivers flooded in 2000, over half a million Bangladeshis took **refuge** in specially built shelters. These are built on high ground.

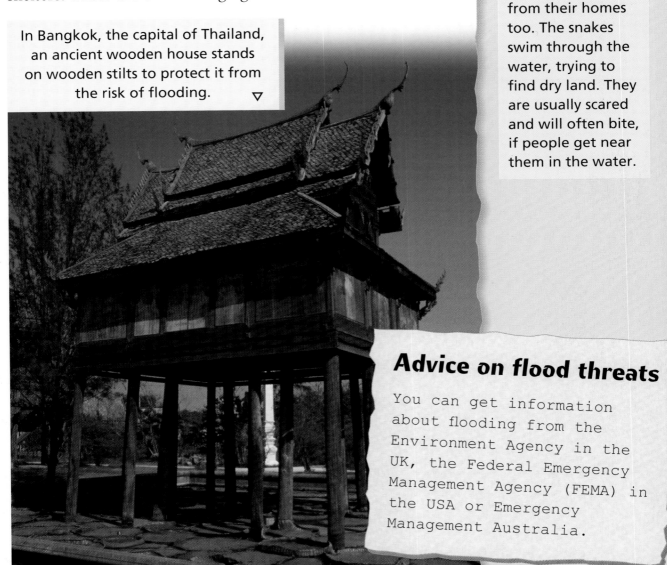

In Bangkok, the capital of Thailand, an ancient wooden house stands on wooden stilts to protect it from the risk of flooding. ▽

## Advice on flood threats

You can get information about flooding from the Environment Agency in the UK, the Federal Emergency Management Agency (FEMA) in the USA or Emergency Management Australia.

refuge    place where you can shelter from danger
stilts    raised legs

## How dams stop floods

The best time to stop a flood is before it starts. **Dams** and **reservoirs** can do this. When there are heavy rains the dams hold back the water in reservoirs. These reservoirs are usually found on **tributary** rivers.

When a big storm hits, the gates of the dams are closed. The dam holds the water back. When the rain stops and the danger of flooding is over, the water is let out slowly. The level of the reservoir behind the dam is lowered to get ready for the next storm.

### A huge saving

If the Tennessee, Ohio and Mississippi Rivers in the USA flooded it would cost about US $200 million in flood damage each year. The Tennessee Valley Authority's system of dams and reservoirs stops this happening.

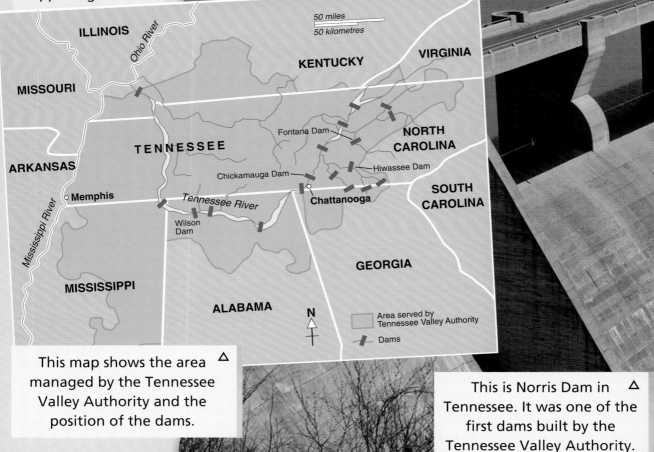

This map shows the area △ managed by the Tennessee Valley Authority and the position of the dams.

This is Norris Dam in △ Tennessee. It was one of the first dams built by the Tennessee Valley Authority.

dam    barrier built to hold back water
economy    wealth of a community

# Tennessee Valley Authority, USA

President Franklin D. Roosevelt set up the Tennessee Valley Authority (TVA) in 1933. This helped the **economy** in one of the poorest regions of the USA. The TVA built more than 30 dams in all. These dams produce electricity as well as control floods.

Big storms are most likely to hit the Tennessee valley in the winter and early spring. The TVA makes room for this water in the flood-storage reservoirs. It lowers their water levels by 31 December each year. The water in these reservoirs can rise and fall by 80 metres.

## Before the TVA

There were many floods in the Tennessee valley before the dams were built. These floods washed away the soil. This caused problems for farmers. Hundreds of people died and thousands more lost their homes and farms. The city of Chattanooga, Tennessee, USA flooded every year.

This is the Tennessee River △ at Chattanooga, USA in the early 1860s. The town is on a bend in the river and used to flood easily.

reservoir    artificial or natural lake that stores water for people to use
tributary    small river flowing into a larger one

## The Mississippi

The Mississippi is one of the greatest rivers in the USA. It has a history of terrible floods. Over the centuries people have tried to protect themselves from its floods. At first the local authorities tried to keep the river in its course, just by building **levees** or **embankments**. But major floods still happened. The worst flood was in 1927. It killed at least 250 people and drove nearly 650,000 from their homes.

## A flood too far

In the 1927 flood the levees broke in 120 separate places. The US government took over the job of flood control. They built **dams, reservoirs, diversion channels** and embankments to control the river.

MINNESOTA
WISCONSIN
IOWA
ILLINOIS
Mississippi River
MISSOURI
KENTUCKY
TENNESSEE
ARKANSAS ○ Memphis
MISSISSIPPI
LOUISIANA
New Orleans ○
MEXICO

N

500 miles
500 kilometres

Gulf of
Mexico

embankment   raised barrier along a riverbank, often called a levee

## Still untamed

The Mississippi is still not completely controlled. Heavy rains in 1993 led to the worst disaster since 1927. The river and its **tributaries** flooded in Iowa, Wisconsin, Illinois and Missouri. Fifty people died and the floods caused US $12 billion of damage.

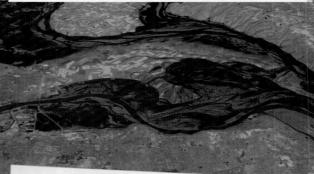

A **satellite** image shows where the Mississippi (top left), Missouri (centre) and Illinois (top centre) rivers met during the 1993 floods. The red patch in the centre shows dry land where the ▽ floodwaters have gone down.

△ In Louisiana, USA, a flood control management centre helps to channel the waters of a branch of the Mississippi River.

*Grafton, Illinois, 1 August 1993*

# Mississippi misery

There is no let-up in sight for victims of the Mississippi flood. Almost 40,000 square kilometres (15,000 square miles) in nine states are now under water. Scientists blame the disaster on months of heavy rain. More than 100,000 homes have been damaged since the start of the flooding.

# Weird weather

**True or false?**

El Niño is a rare event.

Answer: False.

El Niño is a regular part of the world's weather system, although scientists cannot predict it. El Niño may happen every four to eight years.

## El Niño

There is more flooding around the world in some years than in others. Scientists think the changes in the world's weather are linked to the El Niño effect. These changes are felt worldwide. Places where there is usually heavy rain may suffer **drought**. In other regions extra rainfall starts flooding.

## What is El Niño?

El Niño is a change in the flow of ocean **currents** in the Pacific Ocean. Normally the winds and the surface currents of the Pacific Ocean flow westwards. They carry warm water away from South America. When the winds and surface currents change direction an El Niño event happens. The warm waters come much closer to the coasts of North and South America. The ocean waters in this area are sometimes as hot as 27°C. This is three times hotter than their normal temperature.

△ A **satellite** image of the Earth shows the warm-water current linked to El Niño. It is the red band pointed toward the Pacific coast of South America.

current   flow of air or water

## What happens?

When it is an El Niño year heavy rain falls on the South American **coast**. This is because the wind blows rain clouds towards this coast rather than away from it. These lands are usually deserts and the rains make them green. On the far side of the world, the opposite effect happens. The **monsoon** winds are weak. Usually these bring much needed rain to southern Asia. But if they fail the result can be disastrous. There is no rain. Crops fail and there is **famine**.

In February 1998, heavy rains caused by El Niño caused the River Cuyama to flood. It swept away part of a road near the town of Santa Maria, California, USA. ◁

### El Niño

Some effects of the 1997–98 El Niño were:

- Floods in Kenya, Somalia, South Africa, China, Ecuador and Peru

- Droughts in Indonesia, eastern Australia, Mexico, Central America and the southern USA

- The warmest winter on record in Alaska and western Canada

- Record January and February rainfall in the rest of the USA

- The earliest monsoon rains in India in 97 years.

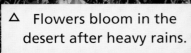

△ Flowers bloom in the desert after heavy rains.

**drought**   when rain or snow fall is far below normal

## Are floods getting worse?

The number of floods every year is going up. There were 6 major flood disasters around the world in the 1950s, 7 in the 1960s, 8 in the 1970s, 18 in the 1980s and 26 in the 1990s.

## Warmer, wetter world

**Global warming** may be one reason for the growing number of floods. People are burning more coal, oil and other fuels. We are pumping harmful gases into the **atmosphere**, like carbon dioxide. These gases trap the sun's heat inside the Earth's atmosphere. This is like the glass roof of a greenhouse capturing warmth. Global warming creates a warmer, wetter world. It causes more rain to fall in some parts of the world. This makes flooding more likely. Ice in the Arctic and Antarctic regions melts because of warmer temperatures. This raises sea levels.

### Building up problems

Paving over an area of ground stops rain from soaking into the soil. Two to six times more water runs off a paved surface compared to bare soil. This means that towns and cities can flood quicker because the water runs straight into rivers.

atmosphere   layer of gases that surrounds the Earth

## Water under control

Governments now realize that they have to spend more money on flood defences. They are building **dams** and **diversion channels** to control floods. Farmers should manage the land so that the risk of flooding is reduced. If farmland is flooded, valuable animals and crops may be lost. **Fertile** soil could be washed away. Developers should only build on brownfield sites. These are areas that have already been built upon. Green fields are needed to soak up extra rain. Water keeps our planet alive. We just need to make sure it is under control.

## Counting the cost

The most costly years for flood damage in the USA in the 20th century were (in US dollars):
1993 $20,463 million
1972 $16,655 million
1951 $12,386 million
1937 $12,261 million
1913 $11,205 million
1927 $11,035 million

### Wonderful wetlands

Wetlands are near rivers and **coasts** and they often flood. They are important for wildlife and they soak up flood water like a sponge. If houses and roads are built in these areas the water has nowhere to go and the flood spreads much further.

# Find out more

## Organizations

### The Weather Channel

This website run by the USA's television weather channel has a weather encyclopedia, plus news, **forecasts** and historical information about weather.
www.weather.com

### BBC Weather

Here you will find forecasts, news and features all about the weather.
www.bbc.co.uk/weather

### BBC News

This is a useful site for news about **droughts** and other extreme weather events.
www.news.bbc.co.uk

### TVA

This site tells you all about the Tennessee Valley Authority.
www.tvakids.com

## Books

*Disasters in Nature: Floods*
Catherine Chambers (Heinemann Library, 2000)
*Nature on the Rampage: Floods*
Tami Deedrick (Raintree, 2004)

## World Wide Web

If you want to find out more about floods, you can search the Internet using keywords like these:

- floods +news +[date you are interested in]
- tsunamis +flood
- El Niño

Find your own keywords by using ideas from this book. Use the search tips on the next page to help you find the most useful websites.

## Search tips

There are billions of pages on the Internet, so it can be difficult to find exactly what you are looking for. For example, if you just type in 'water' on a search engine like Google, you'll get a list of millions of web pages. These tips will help you find useful websites more quickly:

- Decide exactly what you want to find out about first
- Use simple keywords instead of whole sentences
- Use two to six keywords in a search, putting the most important words first
- Be precise. Use names of people, places or things when you can.
- If your keywords are made up of two or more words that go together, put quote marks around them, for example "water shortage"
- Use the + sign to join keywords together, for example weather +disaster
- Adding +KS3 to your keywords may help you find web pages at the right level.

## Where to search

### Search engine

A search engine looks through millions of web pages and lists all the sites that match the words in the search box. They can give thousands of links, but the best matches are at the top of the list, on the first page. Try **www.bbc.co.uk**

### Search directory

A search directory is more like a library of websites that have been sorted by a person instead of a computer. You can search by keyword or subject and browse through the different sites in the same way you would look through books on a library shelf. A good example is **www.yahooligans.com**

# Glossary

**air pressure**   force of the air pressing down on the Earth

**atmosphere**   layer of gases that surrounds the Earth

**bedrock**   hard layer of rock that lies under the soil

**broadcast**   give out information on the radio, television or the Internet

**canyoning**   sport of climbing and swimming up or down gorges

**catchment area**   area of land drained by a river

**civilization**   well-developed social system

**cloudburst**   sudden heavy rainstorm

**coast**   area where the land meets the sea

**coastal defence**   system to protect the coast from the sea

**condense**   when a gas turns into a liquid

**crystal**   solid with atoms arranged in a regular pattern

**current**   flow of air or water

**cyclone**   name given to a hurricane in the southern hemisphere

**dam**   barrier built to hold back water

**death toll**   number of people who died

**deposition**   when material is left in a place by rivers, seas, glaciers or winds

**developed country**   rich country with good living conditions, like Australia, Britain and the USA

**developing country**   poor country, that is trying to become richer and improve its living conditions

**diversion channel**   channel dug alongside a river to drain floodwater

**drought**   when rain or snow fall is far below normal

**dyke**   long wall of earth built to keep water out

**earthquake**   movement of the Earth's surface

**economy**   wealth of a community

**electrocute**   pass electricity through the body

**embankment**   raised barrier along a riverbank, often called a levee

**emergency services**   police, fire and ambulance services

**erosion**   wearing away of soil or rock by water or wind

**evaporate**   when a liquid turns into a gas

**eyewitness**   person who can tell about an event from personal experience

**famine**   long-term shortage of food

**fault line**   crack in the Earth's crust

**fertile**   soil that can grow good crops

**fertilizer**   chemical that gives plants substances necessary for growth

**flash flood**   quickly developing flood

**flaw**   fault or weakness

**forecast**   give information about something that might happen

**foundations**   heavy base that a building stands on

**global warming**   way that the Earth's climate is warming up

**gorge** narrow valley with steep sides

**groundwater** water that soaks into the ground

**hurricane** huge, swirling storm with winds of more than 118 kilometres (73 miles) per hour

**insurance** agreement to provide money in case of a disaster

**lagoon** lake connected to the sea

**landslide** rocks and earth sliding down a hillside

**levee** raised barrier along a riverbank

**low-lying** land that is very close to or below the level of the sea

**meander** bend in the course of a river

**meltwater** water that has come from melted ice or snow

**mineral** natural, solid substance that does not come from an animal or a plant

**monitor** check something regularly

**monsoon** rainy season in some tropical countries

**mouth** where a river flows into the sea

**nutrient** substance needed for living things to grow

**paddy** waterlogged field where rice is grown

**particle** very small piece of a substance

**plain** flat lands

**polluted** dirty, containing harmful substances

**precipitation** rain, snow or hail falling from clouds to the ground

**refuge** place where you can shelter from danger

**reservoir** artificial or natural lake that stores water for people to use

**satellite** object that moves around the Earth in space

**sewer** large underground pipe for carrying away waste water

**silt** soil particles carried by a river

**source** where a river starts

**stilts** raised legs

**stranded** stuck, or washed aground

**surge** sudden rush of water

**survival** escaping death

**survivor** person who escapes death

**tide** regular rising and falling of the sea. This happens twice a day.

**torrent** powerful flow of water

**transpiration** when plants give off water vapour through their leaves

**transportation** when material is carried by water or wind

**tributary** small river flowing into a larger one

**tsunami** giant wave set off by an undersea earthquake or volcanic eruption

**volume** amount of space taken up by a solid, liquid or gas

**water cycle** movement of water between the air, land and sea

**water vapour** water in the form of a gas

**weather station** base for recording the weather

# Index

# Titles in the *Turbulent Planet* series include:

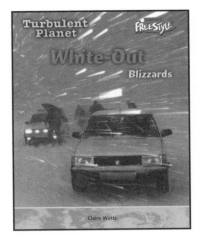

Hardback          1 844 43625 X

Hardback          1 844 43622 5

Hardback          1 844 43626 8

Hardback          1 844 43623 3

Hardback          1 844 43624 1

Find out about the other titles in this series on our website www.raintreepublishers.co.uk